# Johann Sebastian Bach

## Overtures Nos. 3–4
### BWV 1068–1069

Edited by / Herausgegeben von
Harry Newstone

Urtext

**EULENBURG**

EAS 114
ISBN 3-7957-6514-5
ISMN M-2002-2336-1

© 2006 Ernst Eulenburg & Co GmbH, Mainz
for Europe excluding the British Isles
Ernst Eulenburg Ltd, London
for all other countries
Urtext edition based on Eulenburg Study Score ETP 818 and 861
CD ℗ 1989 & © 1997 Naxos Rights International Ltd

Ernst Eulenburg Ltd
48 Great Marlborough Street
London W1F 7BB

# Contents / Inhalt

Overture No. 4 in D major BWV 1069

Bourrée I d.c.

Menuet I d.c.

# Preface

From early in the 17th century until the form engaged the interest of Johann Sebastian Bach, various composers had contributed to the development of the orchestral suite, notably and one of the first, Johann Rosenmüller (c.1619–1684), a predecessor of Bach's at the Thomasschule in Leipzig where he was appointed assistant master in 1642 and where, three years later, he published his first work – a collection of instrumental dances entitled 'Paduanen, Alemanden, Couranten, Balletten, Sarabanden mit 3 Stimmen und ihren Basso pro Organo'.

Other German composers, among them Johann Caspar Ferdinand Fischer (c.1665–1746) whose Op. 1 of 8 Overture-Suites 'Journal de printemps' was published in 1695, and later Georg Philipp Telemann (1681–1767) and Johann Friedrich Fasch (1688–1758) also produced instrumental suites of dances. Fasch, who was to become a scholar at the Thomasschule under Bach's immediate predecessor, Johann Kuhnau (1660–1722), wrote a number of orchestral suites in emulation of his admired Telemann and behind so many of his German contemporaries can be discerned the masterful presence of Jean-Baptiste Lully (1632–1687), not least in the innovation of preceding his dances with an imposing 'Ouverture' from which the form eventually took its name. Fasch, later to go into the service of Count Morzin of Lukavec, Bohemia, (who was in 1759 to give Joseph Haydn his first Music-Directorship) was much admired by Bach who hand-copied a number of Fasch's orchestral suites.

From Bach himself, only four such suites have come down to us although Heinrich Besseler who, with Hans Grüss, edited these works for the *Neue Bach Ausgabe* (NBA), suggest that there may well have been others, now lost, a proposition rejected by Werner Breig in a more recent article on the Bach Suites (in: *The Cambridge Companion to Bach*, 1997, p133). Of the four survivors, only sets of parts (some in Bach's hand) and some copyists' scores are extant, the original autograph scores having disappeared. It would seem that we owe a good deal of our limited knowledge of the Suites Nos. 2, 3 and 4 to the diligence of Christian Friedrich Penzel (1737–1801) who was a student at the Thomasschule from 1751 (the year after Bach's death) and who made copies of Bach manuscripts he found there.

Thus, neither the dates nor the order of composition of the suites can be established with any certainty. The NBA editors suggest that they were composed in the order by which we know them today with the following approximate dates: No. 1 (BWV 1066) 1718, No. 2 (BWV 1067) 1721, No. 3 (BWV 1068) 1722, and No. 4 (BWV 1069) 1723. This would place the suites (or 'Ouverturen' as Bach called them), like the Brandenburg Concertos, in the composer's Cöthen period at which time No. 4 lacked the trumpets and timpani which were added in Leipzig at Christmas 1725 when the first movement was adapted for the opening chorus of the Cantata BWV 110, *Unser Mund sei voll Lachens*. It is possible that the trumpet parts and timpani of the Suite No. 3 were also added later in Leipzig but there is no direct evidence to support this. Breig even suggests that the Suite No. 3 may originally have been written for strings only (CD-liner-notes: Hyperion CDD22002, 1991).

An alternative and quite different chronology for these works is proposed by Stephen Daw, placing the Suite No. 3 in its original version first in order of composition 'by 1724' and the fourth suite in its first version, and the Suite No. 1, 'by the end of 1724', the final version of No. 4 being completed 'c.1729', and the Suite No. 3 'adapted to form its final version' between 'c.1729–31'. '[…] we have no evidence to indicate – as has often been stated –', writes Daw, 'that any of these works were composed before Bach's arrival in Leipzig in May 1723'. Breig supports this possibility and points out that all the surviving sources for the suites originated in Leipzig and proposes the following chronology: 'The principal source of Suite No. 1 […] almost certainly dates from his first year in office; in its original form, Suite No. 4 […] must have been completed before Christmas 1725; Suite No. 3 […] survives in a set of parts dating from 1731; and Suite No. 2 […] survives in an MS from around 1738/9.'

# Overture (Suite) No. 3 in D major, BWV 1068

**Composed: ca. 1722 in Cöthen**
**Original publisher: not published during the composer's lifetime**
**Instrumentation: 2 oboes – 3 trumpets – timpani – violin 1 and 2, viola, violoncello, double bass – continuo**
**Duration: ca. 20 minutes**

The Suite No. 3, which Breig suggests may originally have been written for strings only, dates, in its final form, from around 1731. Among the sources listed in the NBA's Critical Report (Sources A–D), source A is a set of parts in which the first violin part and the continuo parts of the Bourrée and the Gigue are in Bach's hand, the whole of the second violin is in C. P. E. Bach's hand, the rest of Violin I and continuo were written by Johann Ludwig Krebs (who became Bach's pupil in 1726) and the remaining parts by an unidentified copyist. Our edition is based on sources A, C, and D; source B is a handwritten score with a pencilled figured bass and is textually virtually identical with source A. All of these sources are located in the Staatsbibliothek zu Berlin – Preußischer Kultubesitz, Musikabteilung mit Mendelssohn-Archiv.

# Overture (Suite) No. 4 in D major, BWV 1069

**Composed: final version completed in 1725 at the latest;
first version probably dates from Bach's last years in Cöthen,
so therefore before 1723
Original publisher: not published during the composer's lifetime
Other versions: Bach used the first movement in 1725 for his cantata
'Unser Mund sei voll Lachens' BWV 110
Instrumentation: 3 oboes, bassoon – 3 trumpets – timpani – violin 1 and 2,
viola, violoncello, double bass – continuo
Duration: ca. 19 minutes**

The aforementioned Penzel material of the Suite No.4 is, like that of Nos. 2 and 3, located in the Staatsbibliothek zu Berlin Preußischer Kulturbesitz, Musikabteilung mit Mendelssohn Archiv, and, in the absence of a more 'authentic' source, must be taken as the nearest thing to a copy of the missing autograph MS if such actually existed, given the changes that the work went through before it reached this stage. The NBA Critical Report of 1967 lists source A (*Mus. ms. Bach St 160*) as a set of parts. NBA source B (*Mus. ms. Bach P 307 adn. 3*) is a much later score, copied by Anton Werner circa 1839. The oboes are listed in Fischof's catalogue as 3 *Flauti*, though this is presumed to be erroneous as the copyist seemed to have confused the handwritten H and Fl. Source C (*Mus. ms. Bach St 445*) is an incomplete set of parts by an unknown copyist written on paper that can be dated back to Bach's time. Neither of these sources has been used in the preparation of the present new edition. The previous Eulenburg edition by Wilhelm Altmann and dated 1927 has been examined but similarly rejected because it has simply standardized the phrasing without direct reference to the sources from which they derive.

Harry Newstone (adapted)

# Vorwort

Vom Beginn des 17. Jahrhunderts bis zu dem Moment, als sich Johann Sebastian Bach der Orchestersuite zuwandte, hatten schon verschiedene Komponisten zur Entwicklung dieser Gattung beigetragen. Hier ist vor allem Johann Rosenmüller (um 1619–1684) zu nennen, ein Vorgänger Bachs an der Thomasschule in Leipzig. Er wurde dort 1642 stellvertretender Kantor und veröffentlichte drei Jahre später sein erstes Werk – eine Sammlung von instrumentalen Tänzen mit dem Titel *Paduanen, Alemanden, Couranten, Balletten, Sarabanden mit 3 Stimmen und ihren Basso pro Organo*.

Aber auch andere deutsche Komponisten komponierten instrumentale Tanzsuiten; so z. B. Johann Caspar Fischer (um 1665–1746), dessen Opus 1 *Le Journal de printemps* (8 Ouvertüren-Suiten) 1695 gedruckt wurde, und später Georg Philipp Telemann (1681–1767) sowie Johann Friedrich Fasch (1688–1758). Fasch, ein Schüler von Bachs unmittelbarem Vorgänger Johann Kuhnau (1660–1722), schrieb eine Anzahl von Orchestersuiten, in denen er seinem Vorbild Telemann nacheiferte. Bei ihm ist aber auch, wie bei so vielen seiner zeitgenössischen, deutschen Komponistenkollegen, die meisterhafte Präsenz von Jean-Baptiste Lully (1632–1687) erkennbar. Diese zeigt sich nicht zuletzt in der Neuerung, den Tanzsätzen eine imposante 'Ouvertüre' voranzustellen, von der diese Form möglicherweise auch ihren Namen hat. Fasch, der später in die Dienste des Grafen Morzin zu Lukawitz in Böhmen trat (desjenigen Grafen also, der 1759 Joseph Haydn seine erste Musikdirektorenstelle gab), wurde von Bach, der mehrere seiner Orchestersuiten abschrieb, sehr bewundert.

Von Bach selbst sind nur vier Orchestersuiten überliefert. Heinrich Besseler, der diese Werke zusammen mit Hans Grüss in der Neuen Bach Ausgabe (NBA) edierte, vermutete allerdings, dass es möglicherweise mehr Werke gegeben habe, die nun aber verschollen seien. Diese These wurde jedoch von Werner Breig in einem Artikel über Bachs Suiten zurückgewiesen (in: *The Cambridge Companion to Bach*, 1997, S. 133). Von den vier überlieferten Werken existieren lediglich Stimmen (einige davon in Bachs Handschrift) sowie einige Partituren, die von Kopisten stammen. Die autographen Partituren sind verschollen. Ein Großteil unseres ohnehin begrenzten Wissens über die Suiten Nr. 2, 3 und 4 scheinen wir dem Eifer Christian Friedrich Penzels (1737–1801) zu verdanken. Er war seit 1751 (dem Jahr nach Bachs Tod) Schüler an der Thomasschule und kopierte die dort von ihm vorgefundenen Manuskripte Bachs.

Deshalb können wir weder über die Entstehungsdaten noch die Kompositionsreihenfolge gesicherte Aussagen machen. Die Herausgeber der NBA vertreten die These, dass sie in der uns heute bekannten Folge komponiert wurden, wobei sie hinsichtlich der Datierung von den folgenden Annäherungswerten ausgingen: Nr. 1 (BWV 1066) 1718, Nr. 2 (BWV 1067) 1721, Nr. 3 (BWV 1068) 1722, Nr. 4 (BWV 1069) 1723. Damit würden die Entstehungszeiten der Suiten (oder „Ouvertüren", wie sie Bach nannte), den Brandenburgischen Konzerten vergleichbar, noch in Bachs Köthener Zeit fallen. Zu diesem Zeitpunkt fehlten in der 4. Suite noch die Trompeten und Pauken. Sie wurden erst Weihnachten 1725 in Leipzig ergänzt, als Bach den ersten Satz für den Eröffnungschor der Kantate BWV 110 *Unser Mund sei voller Lachens* umarbeitete. Es ist ferner möglich, dass auch die Trompeten und Pauken der 3. Suite erst in der Leipziger Zeit ergänzt wurden, doch lassen sich dafür keine direkten Hinweise finden. Breig vermutet sogar, die 3. Suite sei ursprünglich nur für Streicher geschrieben worden (CD-Einführung: Hyperion CDD22002, 1991).

Eine gänzlich davon abweichende Chronologie schlägt Stephen Daw vor: Er setzt die 3. Suite in der Originalfassung als erste der vier Suiten „um 1724" an und die 4. Suite in ihrer ersten Fassung sowie die 1. Suite „gegen Ende 1724". Die Endfassung der 4. Suite sei „ca. 1729" beendet worden und die 3. Suite in ihrer endgültigen Form zwischen „ca. 1729 und 1731". Daws schreibt ferner: „[...] wir haben keinen Beweis dafür, dass – wie oft gesagt wurde – irgendeines dieser Werk vor Bachs Ankunft in Leipzig im Mai 1723 geschrieben wurde." Breig unterstützt diese Hypothese und weist darauf hin, dass alle überlieferten Quellen zu den Orchestersuiten aus Leipzig stammen. Er schlägt folgende Chronologie vor: „Die Hauptquelle der 1. Suite stammt mit ziemlicher Sicherheit aus seinem ersten Jahr in Leipzig. Die 4. Suite muß in ihrer Originalfassung vor Weihnachten 1725 beendet worden sein, die 3. Suite ist in einem Satz Orchesterstimmen von 1731 erhalten, und die 2. Suite ist in einem Manuskript aus dem Jahr 1738/39 überliefert."

# Ouvertüre (Suite) Nr. 3 in D-Dur, BWV 1068

**komponiert: um 1722 in Köthen**
**Originalverlag: zu Lebzeiten des Komponisten nicht gedruckt**
**Orchesterbesetzung: 2 Oboen – 3 Trompeten – Pauken – Violine I und II,**
**Viola, Violoncello, Kontrabass – Basso continuo**
**Spieldauer: etwa 20 Minuten**

Die 3. Suite, von der Breig vermutet, sie sei ursprünglich nur für Streicher geschrieben worden, ist in ihrer endgültigen Fassung auf die Zeit um 1731 zu datieren. Unter den im Kritischen Bericht der NBA verzeichneten Quellen A–D ist Quelle A ein Stimmensatz, dessen Partien der 1. Violine und des Continuos in der *Bourrée* und *Gigue* von Bachs Hand sind. Die übrigen Sätze dieser Stimmen schrieb Johann Ludwig Krebs (der 1726 Bachs Schüler wurde) aus und die gesamte 2. Violinstimme C. Ph. E. Bach, während die übrigen Stimmen von einem unbekannten Kopisten sind. Die vorliegende Edition fußt auf den Quellen A, C und D. Quelle B ist eine handschriftliche Partitur, die eine mit Bleistift notierte Bezifferung des Basses enthält, und nahezu identisch mit Quelle A ist. Alle Quellen befinden sich in der Musikabteilung der Staatsbibliothek zu Berlin – Preußischer Kulturbesitz.

# Ouvertüre (Suite) Nr. 4 in D-Dur, BWV 1069

**komponiert: in der Endfassung spätestens 1725; die Urfassung datiert wahrscheinlich aus der letzten Köthener Zeit, also vor 1723
Originalverlag: zu Lebzeiten des Komponisten nicht gedruckt
Fassungen und Bearbeitungen: Den ersten Satz verwendete Bach für den Einleitungschor der Kantate „Unser Mund sei voll Lachens" BWV 110 aus dem Jahr 1725.
Orchesterbesetzung: 3 Oboen, Fagott – 3 Trompeten – Pauken – Violine I und II, Viola, Violoncello, Kontrabass – Basso continuo
Spieldauer: etwa 19 Minuten**

Das oben erwähnte Penzel-Material der 4. Suite befindet sich wie das der zweiten und dritten in der Staatsbibliothek zu Berlin – Preußischer Kulturbesitz, Musikabteilung mit Mendelssohn Archiv; da man keine „bessere" Quelle kennt, mag es am ehesten als eine Kopie des verschollenen Autographs gelten (falls ein solches tatsächlich existierte), wenn man an die bis dahin vorgenommenen Änderungen denkt. Der Kritische Bericht der NBA von 1967 listet Quelle A (*Mus. ms. Bach St 160*) als Stimmensatz. Die NBA Quelle B (*Mus. ms. Bach P 307 adn. 3*) ist eine viel spätere Partitur, ca. 1839 von Anton Werner abgeschrieben. Die Oboen sind in Fischofs Katalog als drei Flöten angegeben; das wird jedoch als falsch angesehen, da der Schreiber vermutlich das handgeschriebene H und Fl verwechselte. Quelle C (*Mus. ms. Bach St 445*) ist ein unvollkommener Stimmensatz von einem unbekannten Kopisten, dessen Papier auf Bachs Zeit zurückdatiert werden kann. Keine dieser Quellen wurde in der vorliegenden Ausgabe herangezogen. Auch die frühere Eulenburg Edition von Wilhelm Altmann, datiert 1927, wurde zwar untersucht aber abgelehnt; dort war die Phrasierung ohne direkte Quellenreferenz einfach standardisiert worden.

Harry Newstone (neu bearbeitet)
Übersetzung: Ann-Katrin Heimer

# Overture No. 3 in D major

Johann Sebastian Bach
(1685–1750)
BWV 1068

## I. Ouverture

© 2006 Ernst Eulenburg Ltd, London
and Ernst Eulenburg & Co GmbH, Mainz

2

4

6

8

★) See Appendix A p. 40

EAS 114

10

12

★) See Appendix B p. 43

14

16

18

EAS 114

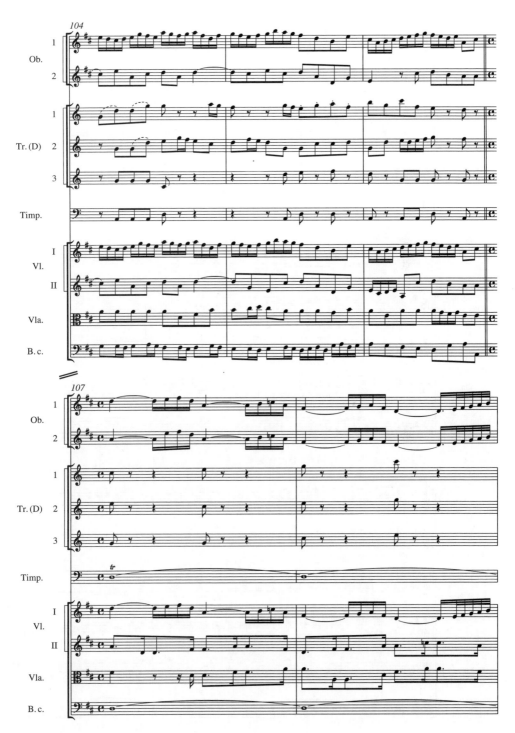

20

22

## II. Air

★) See Appendix C p. 46

24

## III. Gavotte 1

Oboe

Tromba (D)

Timpani

Violino

Viola

Basso continuo

26

EAS 114

[*Fine*]

Gavotte 2

30

Da Capo [III.]

# IV. Bourrée

EAS 114

32

34

## V. Gigue

38

40

# Appendix A: from *D-B* Mus.ms.Bach P1055

42

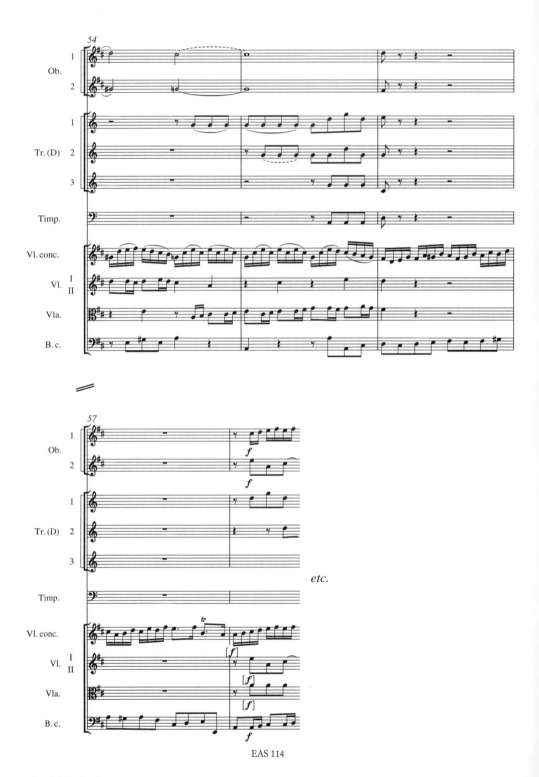

EAS 114

# Appendix B: from *D-B* Mus.ms.Bach P1055

44

# Appendix C: from *D-B* Mus.ms.Bach P1055

## II. Air

# Overture No. 4 in D major

Johann Sebastian Bach
(1685–1750)
BWV 1069

I. Ouverture

49

50

52

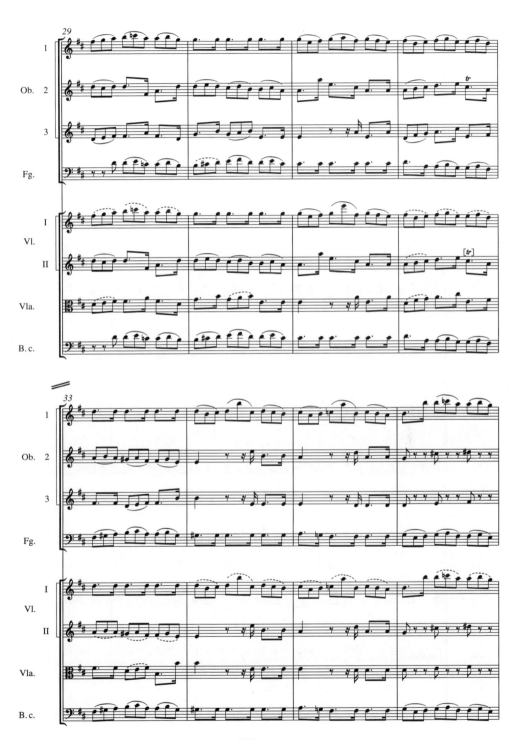

56

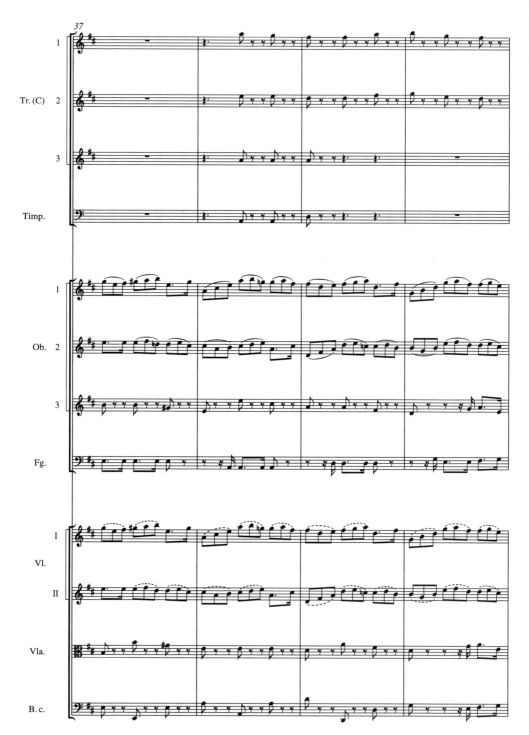

58

EAS 114

60

EAS 114

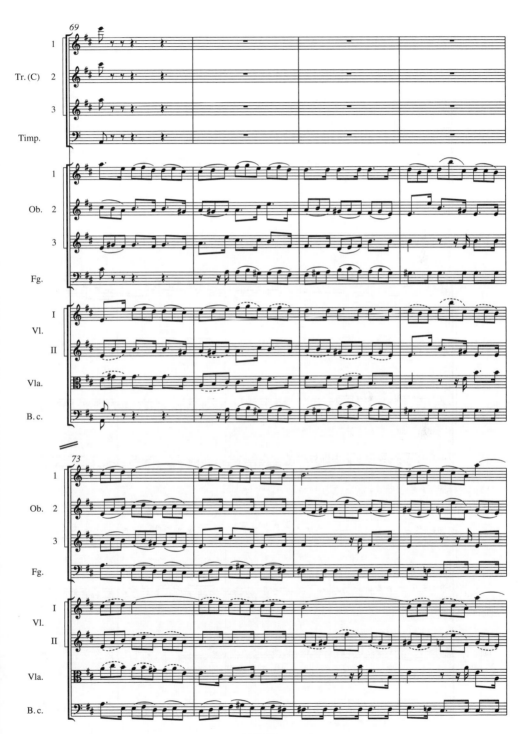

64

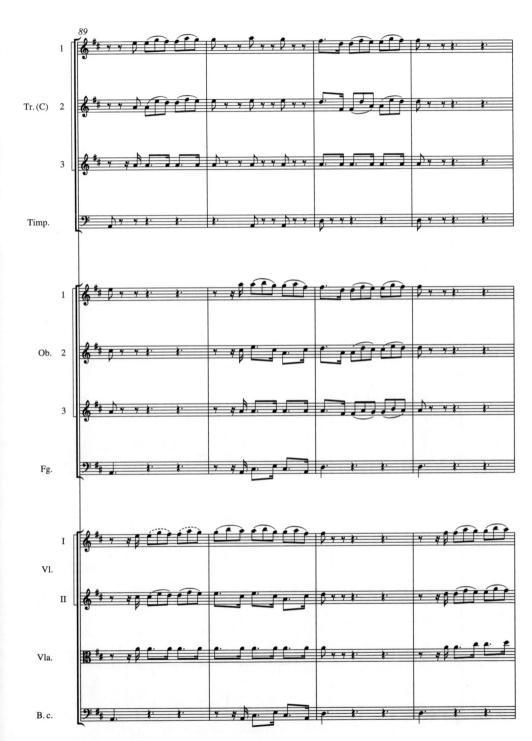

66

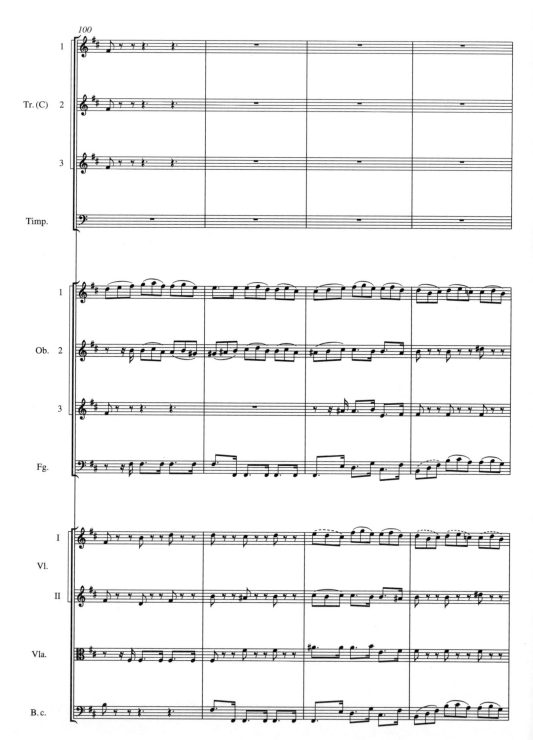

70

71

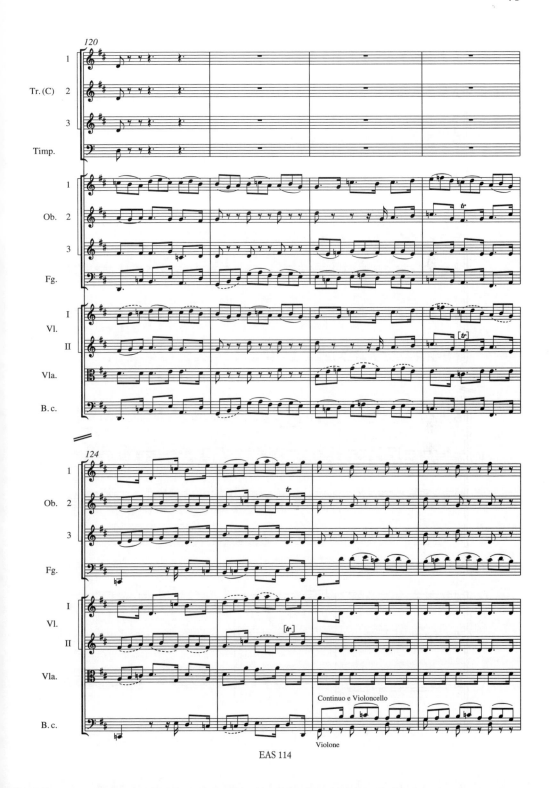

Continuo e Violoncello

Violone

EAS 114

72

74

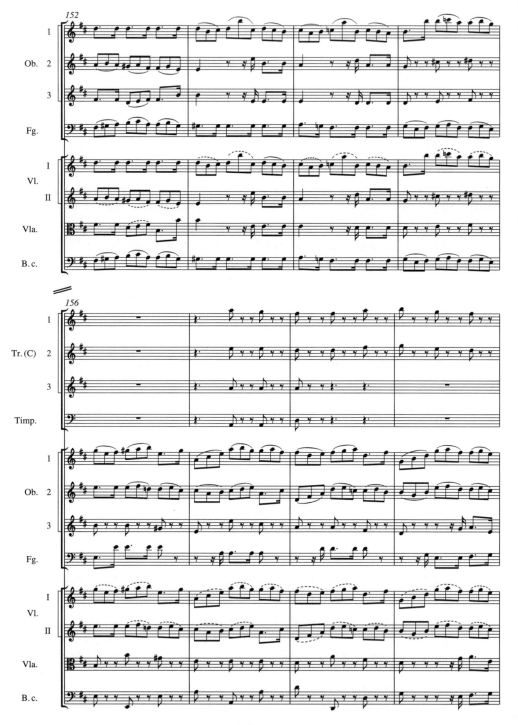

82

## II. Bourrée 1 alternativement

84

## Bourrée 2

86

EAS 114

*Bourrée 1 da capo*

# III. Gavotte

94

### IV. Menuet 1 alternativement

## Menuet 2

*Menuet 1 da capo*

98

## V. Réjouissance

100

EAS 114

104

EAS 114

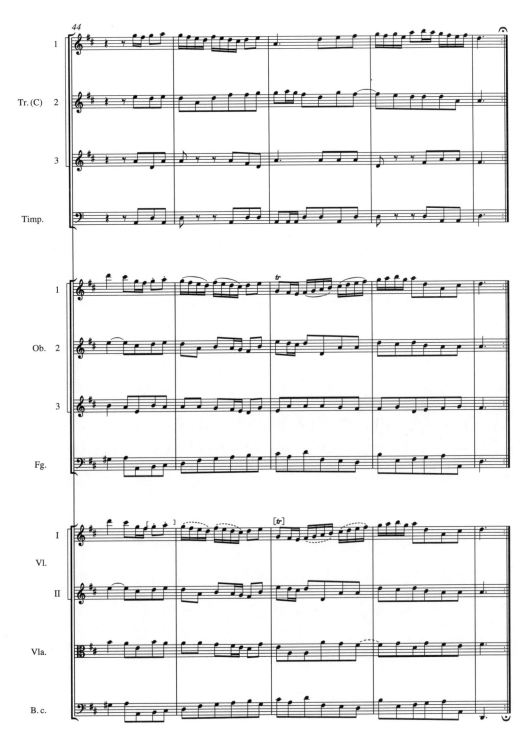

Printed in China